Play Ball

Contents | Page

written by John Lockyer

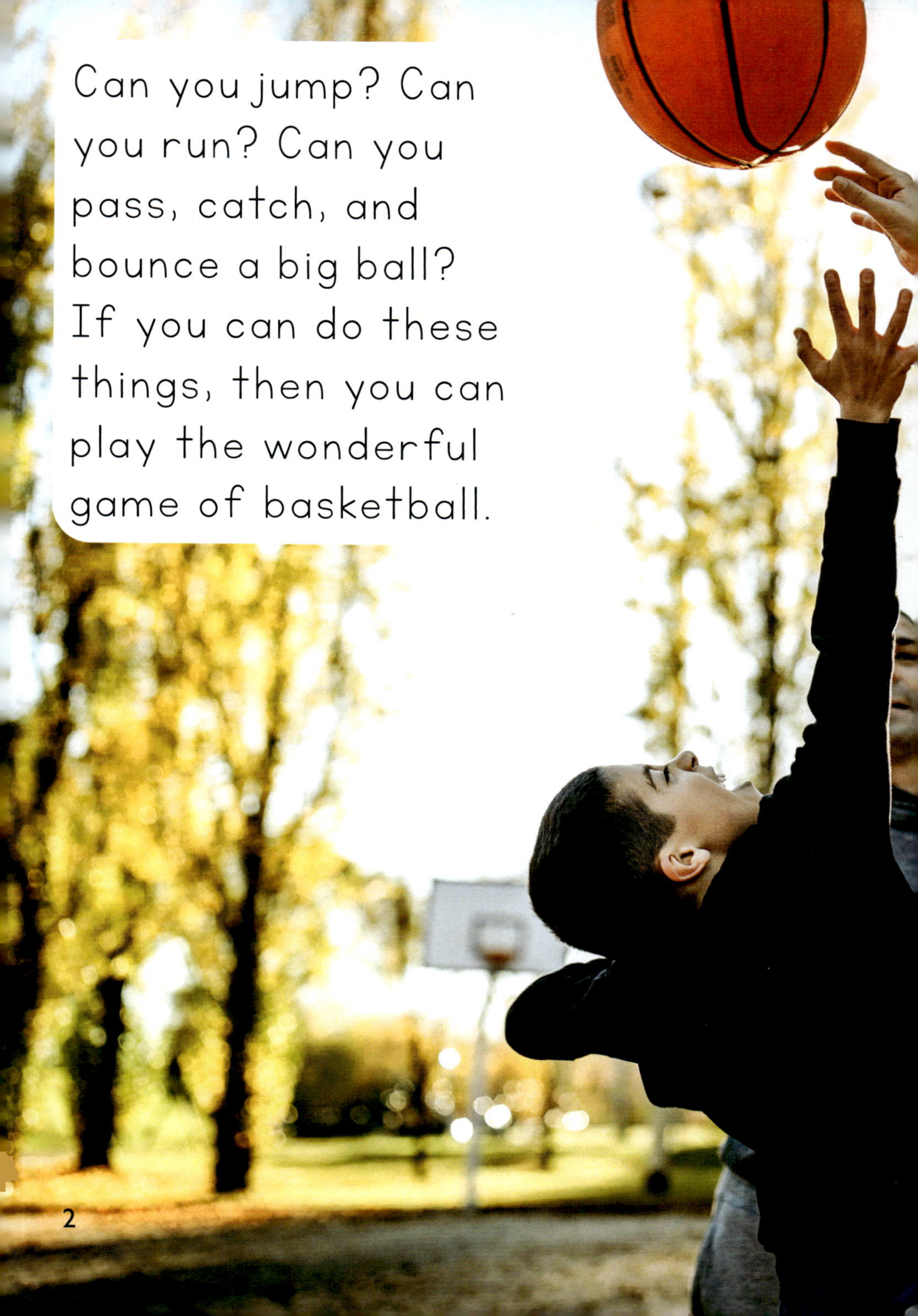

Can you jump? Can you run? Can you pass, catch, and bounce a big ball? If you can do these things, then you can play the wonderful game of basketball.

tip-off

Basketball players must learn useful skills. Shooting is an important skill. Good players can shoot the ball into the basket from anywhere close to the hoop.

shooting

Sometimes a player will miss a shot. When the ball bounces off the backboard, anyone can grab it. This is called a rebound.

There are many different basketball passes: chest pass, bounce pass, overhead pass, and baseball pass.

rebound

Players are defending when they try to stop the other team from scoring. Taking the ball cleanly is the best way to defend.

Playing the game is fun, but there are rules. Each team has five players. The game starts with a tip-off.

The player who has the ball must dribble to move with the ball. If they stop dribbling, then it must be passed to someone else.

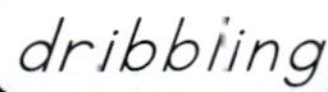

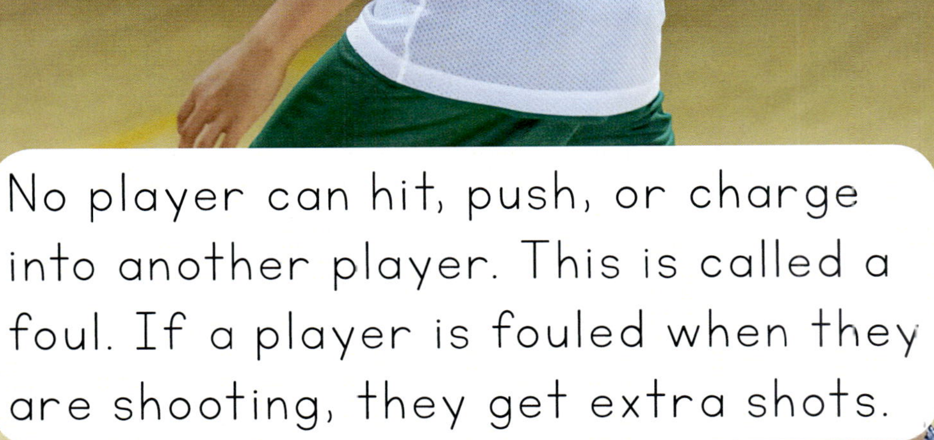

No player can hit, push, or charge into another player. This is called a foul. If a player is fouled when they are shooting, they get extra shots.

Players can get between one and three points. A free-throw is worth one point. A good shot from in front of the three-point line gets two points.

Three points are scored from a basket from behind the three-point line. When the game is over, the winning team is the one with the most points.

Basketball is played by some great players. Their games are played in huge stadiums, where many people come to watch them play. The large crowd always claps and cheers when the players do a slam-dunk.

stadium

Basketball can be played at school, at home, in the gym, or in the park. Play ball!